better together*

* This book is best read together, grownup and kid.

a
kids
book
about

a kids book about CHOICES

by Kyle Quilausing

A Kids Book About
Editor Emma Wolf
Head of Design Rick DeLucco
Publisher Jelani Memory

DK
Senior Production Editor Jennifer Murray
Senior Production Controller Louise Minihane
Managing Editor Hazel Eriksson
Publishing Director Mark Searle

This American Edition, 2026
Published in the United States by DK Publishing,
a Division of Penguin Random House LLC
1745 Broadway, 20th Floor, New York, NY 10019

26 27 28 29 10 9 8 7 6 5 4 3 2 1
001—355685—March/26

First published in Great Britain in 2026 by
Dorling Kindersley Limited, 20 Vauxhall Bridge Road, London SW1V 2SA
A Penguin Random House Company

The authorised representative in the EEA is
Dorling Kindersley Verlag GmbH. Arnulfstr. 124, 80636 Munich, Germany

A CIP catalogue record for this book is available from the British Library

ISBN 978-0-2417-8595-9

Printed and bound in China

www.dk.com

akidsco.com

Interested in bringing Kyle Quilausing to your school or event?
Visit topyouthspeakers.com/kyle

This book was made with Forest Stewardship Council™ certified paper – one small step in DK's commitment to a sustainable future.
Learn more at www.dk.com/uk/information/sustainability

To my Savior, Jesus Christ,
who turned my mess into a mission.

To my children, this book is for you.

To my wife, thank you for standing
by me when I had nothing to give.

Intro
for grownups

Aloha! I'm Uncle Kyle, and I want to share something with you that I've learned in my life: People make choices, and choices make people.

When I was younger, I didn't always make good choices. Some of my choices led me to a very hard place. But it wasn't always like that. I was a hard-working kid who cared about school and his family. Until one day, I learned a lesson I still carry with me and share with everyone I meet:

You're one choice away from a different life.

That's why I'm telling you my story. Because I want YOU to know that no matter where you are, or what has happened, every day is a new chance. The choices you make today shape who you become tomorrow.

So, let's turn the page together and learn how powerful your choices really are.

PEOPLE MAKE AND CHOICES

CHOICES,
MAKE PEOPLE.

My life has been shaped
by the **choices** I've made.

And I believe you are always

ONE CHOICE AWAY FROM A DIFFERENT LIFE.

My name is 

I grew up on the big island of Hawai'i.

At 3 years old,
my parents got divorced.

My mom made the **choice** to take her kids out of a hard situation and move in with her parents.

My grandpa was the chief of police and taught me a lot about life.

He taught me love, rules, responsibility...

AND THE GAME OF GOLF.

The golf course was
just outside of our backyard.

Every free moment I spent at that
golf course—it was my playground.

At the age of 10,
I competed in a golf tournament.

And...

I WON!

At 10 years old, I was a
junior golf state champion.

This qualified me to represent
my state of Hawai'i in the junior
world championship.

This was the first time
I met Tiger Woods. So cool!

I looked over to my left
and there he was.

He looked at me,
I gave him a shaka,
and we went on with our day.

Guess who came first that day? Tiger.

I was now ranked 4th
in the **world** for golf.

I came home, looked out over
that golf course in my backyard,
and I made some goals for myself.

I started making **choices**
to support those goals.

Every day, as soon as the sun came up, I practiced golf.

I got 2 hours of work in by the time my competitors were starting their day.

I kept going until I heard my mom call, "Kyle! School!"

I knew to be a world champion
at golf, I needed to be
a smart player.

So I chose to take school seriously.

I paid attention in class,
I loved my teachers,
I worked hard.

After school,
I did my homework
and then golfed until
the sun went down.

And I did this every day.

By senior year, I came home to find envelopes from colleges all over the place, wanting me to come play golf for them.

MY FUTURE WAS SET, AND IT WAS BRIGHT.

My choices had brought me
to this point, on the edge of
getting everything I ever wanted.

And once those dreams
were close enough to touch,
I made different **choices**.

My ego GREW
and I started acting
like a totally different person.

I stopped caring about school,
I stopped treating my teachers
with respect.

They tried to help me,
but I was too selfish to hear them.

And then...

I MADE A B

AD CHOICE.

A really, really bad **choice**.

And it would change my life forever.

I got expelled from school.

So quickly, everything I had worked for slipped through my fingers.

Because of that one bad **choice**.

That's how fast
your **choices** can
change your life.

HAVE YOU EVER MADE A CHOICE YOU REGRET?

AFTER THAT, I MADE A LOT OF BAD CHOICES.

I was on the news.

Not because I beat Tiger Woods
in a golf tournament.

Not because I became a millionaire
and bought a beautiful house.

But because I was
"Hawai'i's Most Wanted."

I was a criminal.
And ultimately, I got caught.

I spent a month in the jail
right by my house.

And...I planned my escape.

Another bad **choice**.

Now, I was an escaped fugitive.

And when I was caught again,
I was put in a small isolation cell.

ALL BY

MYSELF.

My hair grew longer, my skin
got paler, and things felt so dark.

In that small space, the only place
I could go was down to my knees.

I hadn't grown up
going to church
or learning about God,
but I called out anyway.

I asked for help, I asked for
forgiveness, and when I stood up,
everything had changed for me.

I was still in that small cell,
but I had a new sense of hope.

I WAS GIVEN THE

TO MAKE NEW

BETTER

OPPORTUNITY CHOICES, CHOICES.

The rest of my time in prison was still so hard and painful, but I had this new motivation to make it through.

I came home without a penny in my pocket, but with a new heart and a new mindset.

I've dedicated my life since then to helping kids (just like you) know the power of their **choices**.

You will make so many **choices** in your life.

I share my story to show
how **choices** affect you
and also the people you love.

You can make a **choice**
in a moment that affects you
for the rest of your life.

I don’t say this to scare you,
but so you understand
how much power you have.

So, what do you do with that power?

STAY HUMBLE

AND **PRAY.** I do that every day.

STAY HUMBLE MEANS

to not think too much of yourself.

To know that you're just human.

And that a bad decision
can really hurt your life.

TO PRAY MEANS

to ask for help.

For me, I ask God, my friends,
and trusted grownups for help.

Who in your life can you ask for help?

MAKING GOOD ISN'T

Sometimes it's because
you don't know what to do.

CHOICES ALWAYS EASY.

Other times it's because
it's just hard to do.

In Hawai'i we have
a lot of waterfalls.

Before we jump,
we always do one thing.

We check how deep the water is.
If it's too shallow, we don't jump
because we'll get hurt.

When you have
a **choice** to make,
you can make a

GOOD CHOICE

or a **BAD CHOICE.**

Make sure to check first.

Is it safe? Is it good? Is it right?

Hard days will come.
That's a part of life.

But they will pass,
just like a storm.

Know your value and persevere.

Each day is a new chance to make smart **choices**.

STAY **HUMBLE,** AND

CHOOSE WISELY.

Outro
for grownups

People make choices, and choices make people. And you? You're always one choice away from a different life.

That's the truth. Every choice matters, big or small. Every choice helps shape the person you're becoming.

I know you've got what it takes to choose wisely. I believe in you.

So, when the next choice comes? Remember these words: One choice can change everything.

Cheeeeeeeeehuuuuuu (Mahalo),
Uncle Kyle

About The Author

Kyle Quilausing (he/him) is a Native Hawaiian from Hilo, Hawai'i, who grew up golfing alongside Eldrick "Tiger" Woods. Today, he is a national motivational speaker dedicated to helping people understand the power of their choices.

After learning firsthand how one decision can change everything, Kyle made it his life's mission to reach as many lives as possible. He speaks to both kids and grownups across the country, sharing his message in schools, treatment centers, prisons, churches, and community events. Whether he is speaking to a 9-year-old student or a 45-year-old inmate, his heart remains the same: to remind people that they are always one choice away from a different life. Through this book, Kyle hopes to reach kids early and inspire them to stay on the right path.

@stayhumbleprayhawaii 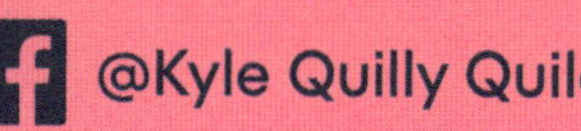 @Kyle Quilly Quilausing